JAZZ STANDARDS

CD Produced by Ed Roscetti and Jamie Findlay
Recorded and Mixed by Ed Roscetti at Groovetoons, Studio City, California

ISBN 978-1-4234-3043-8

HAL•LEONARD®
CORPORATION
7777 W. BLUEMOUND RD. P.O. BOX 13819 MILWAUKEE, WI 53213

Visit Hal Leonard Online at
www.halleonard.com

CONTENTS

JAMIE FINDLAY

Photo by James Murphy

Jamie Findlay began playing guitar at the age of eight. He has performed almost all types of music: pop, country western, swing, jazz, Brazilian, Latin, folk, and classical, both as a solo performer and in larger ensembles. He's performed with Frank Sinatra, Jr., Dan Seals, Dash Crofts, Russell Ferrante, Alex Acuña, Howard Roberts, Joe Diorio, Ralph Towner, and Red Grammer; has recorded with Buddy Childers, Tierney Sutton, Steve Huff-steter, and his own quartet, the Acoustic Jazz Quartet, among others. He has traveled and performed throughout Europe, Southeast Asia, Brazil, China, Japan, Central America, and in most of the U.S. He is an active music educator, having given guitar workshops all over the world and has contributed to several guitar publications. After several years teaching in the Studio/Jazz Guitar department at USC, Jamie is currently an instructor at Musicians Institute in Hollywood.

Jamie is extremely happy to play a Heritage Sweet 16, a Shoenberg Soloist, and a Ronald Ho Classical. He enthusiastically uses La Bella strings, Seymour Duncan pickups, and the D-Tar Acoustic pre-amp, and loves the sound of his Framus Acoustifier amp.

16.50

All of Me

Words and Music by Seymour Simons and Gerald Marks

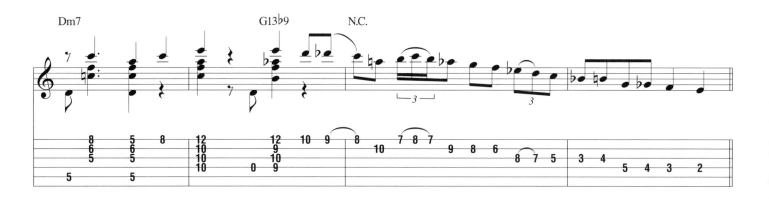

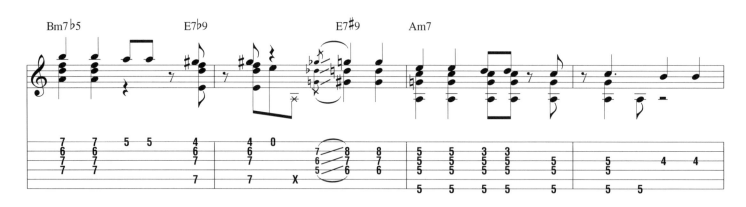

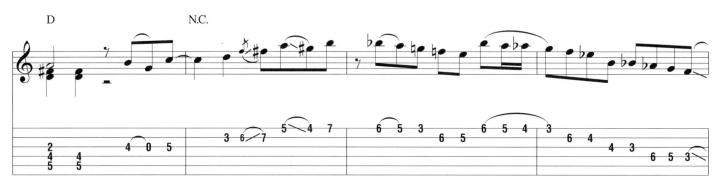

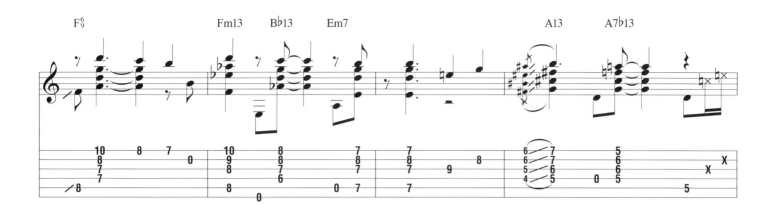

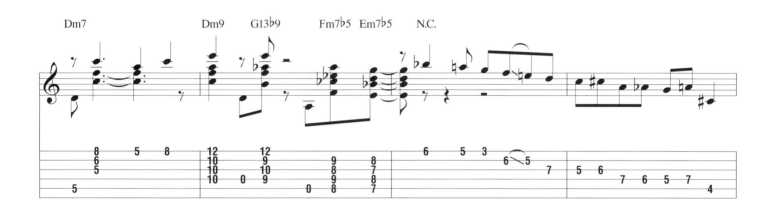

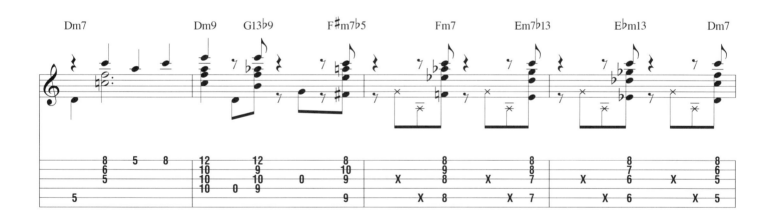

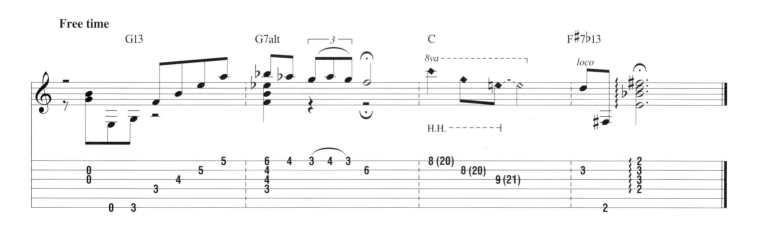

Blame It on My Youth

Words by Edward Heyman
Music by Oscar Levant

Edelweiss

from THE SOUND OF MUSIC
Lyrics by Oscar Hammerstein II
Music by Richard Rodgers

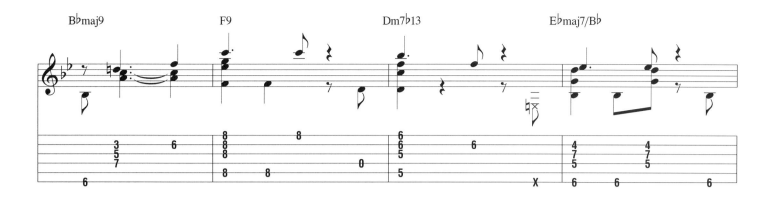

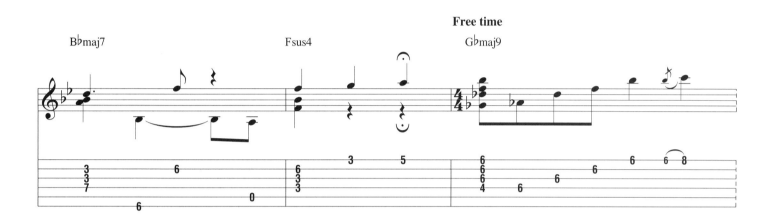

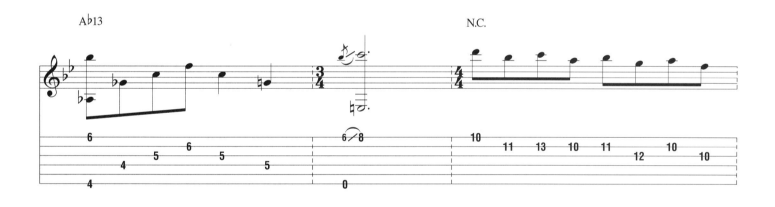

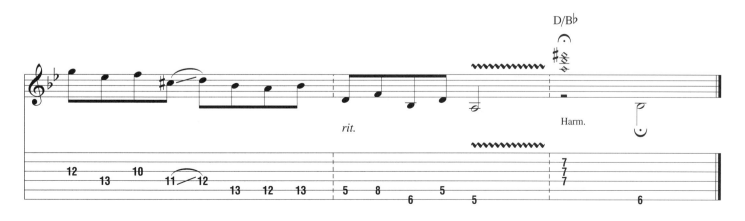

If I Loved You

from CAROUSEL

Lyrics by Oscar Hammerstein II
Music by Richard Rodgers

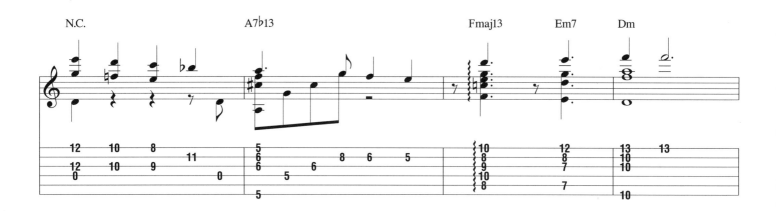

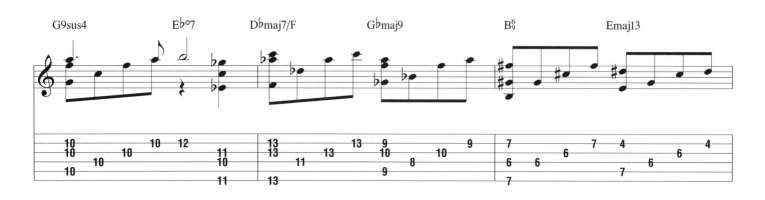

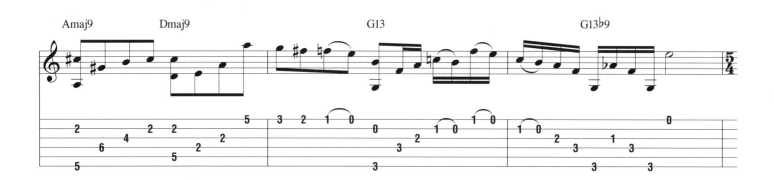

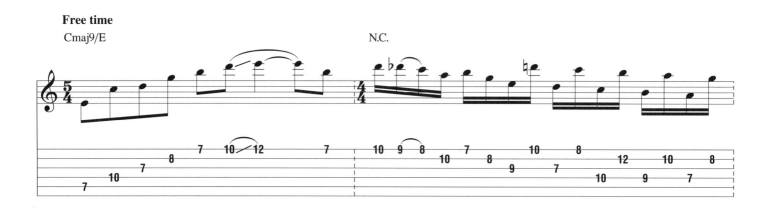

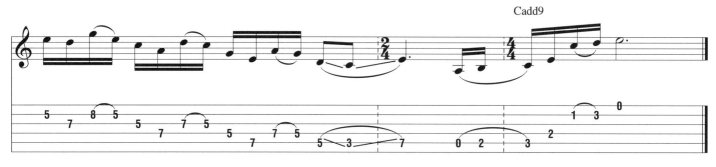

It Might as Well Be Spring

from STATE FAIR

Lyrics by Oscar Hammerstein II
Music by Richard Rodgers

B

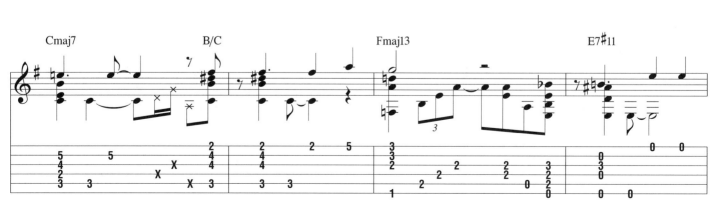

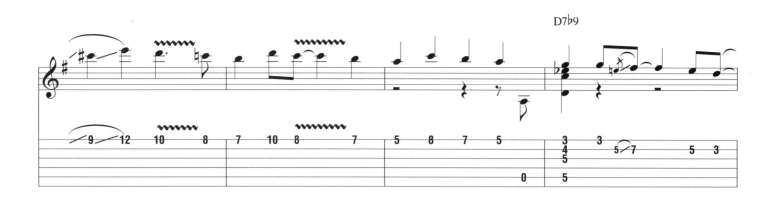

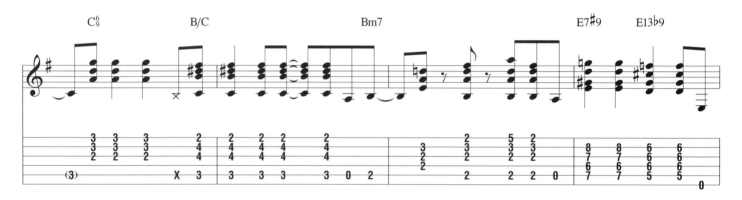

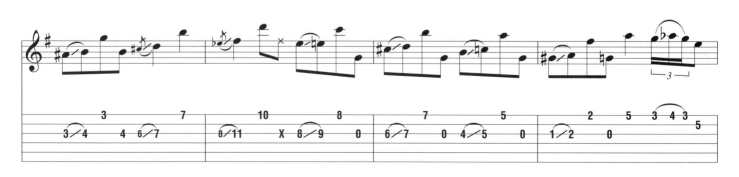

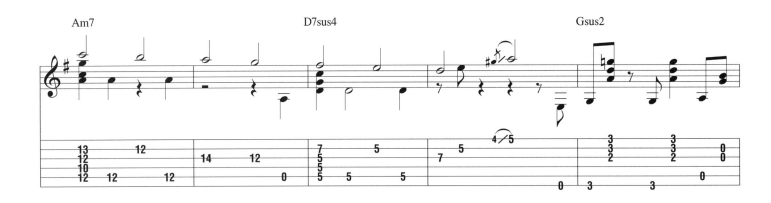

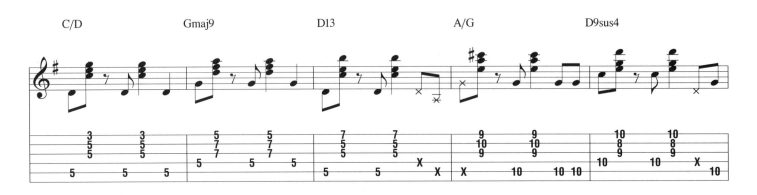

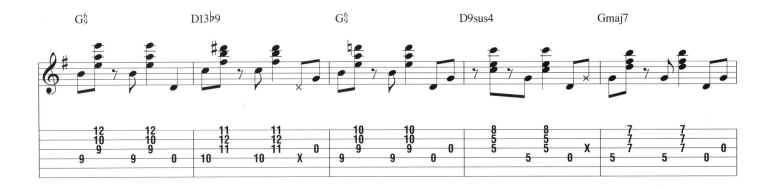

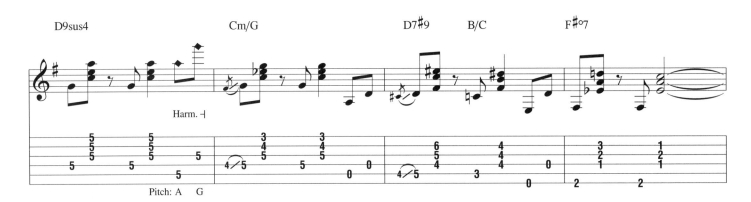

Misty

Music by Erroll Garner

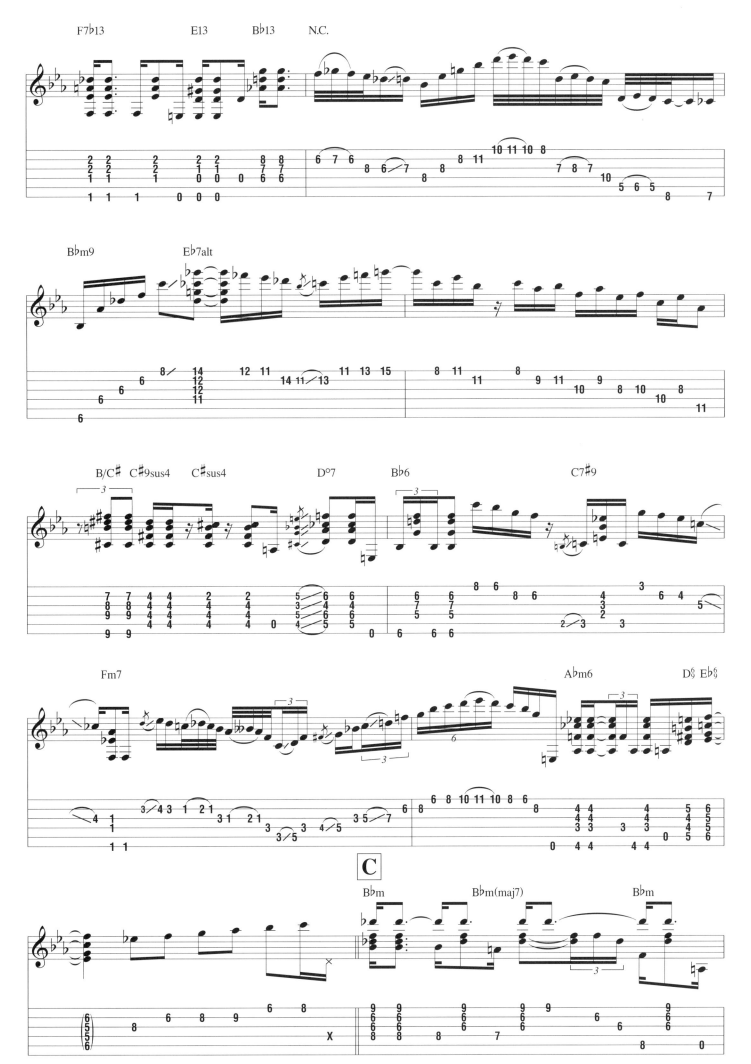

My Favorite Things

from THE SOUND OF MUSIC

Lyrics by Oscar Hammerstein II
Music by Richard Rodgers

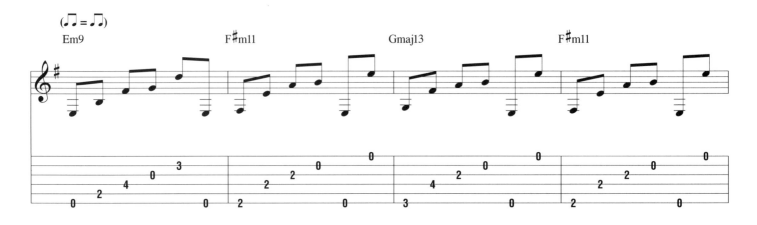

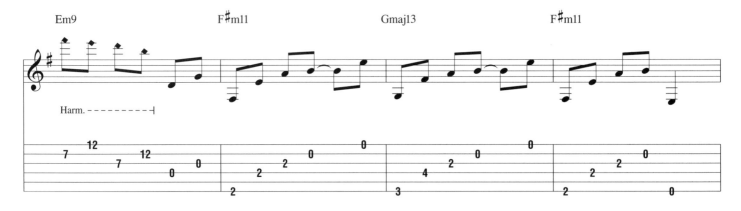

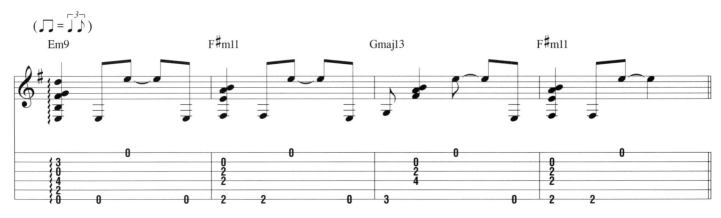

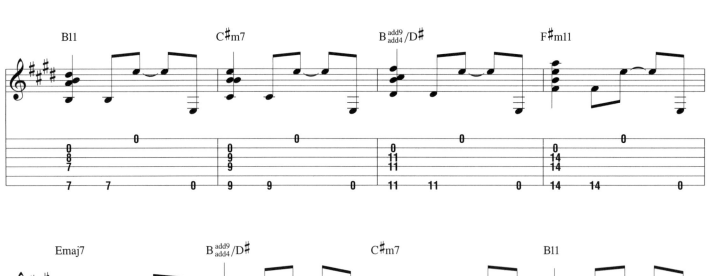

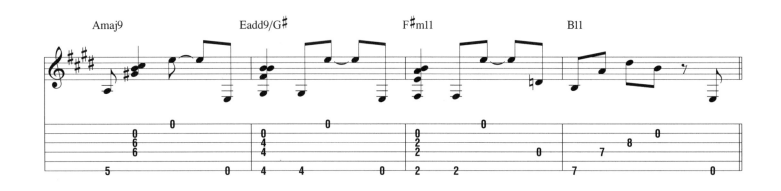
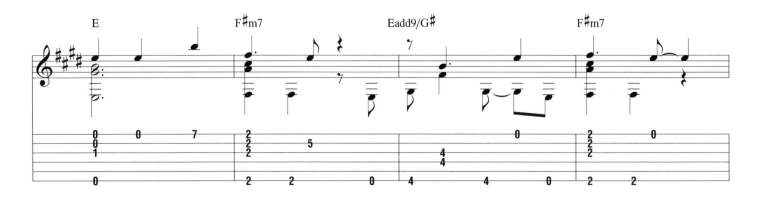
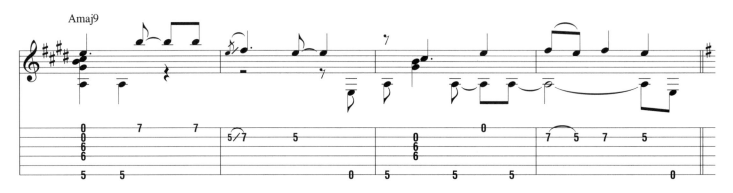

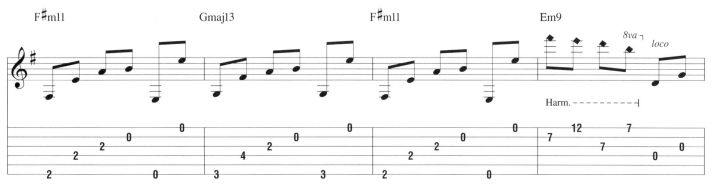

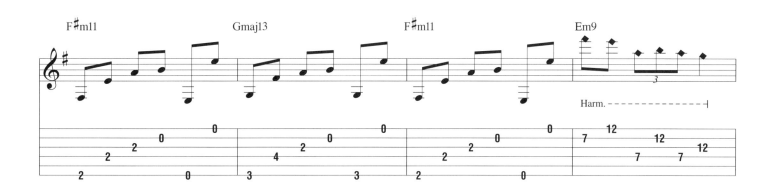

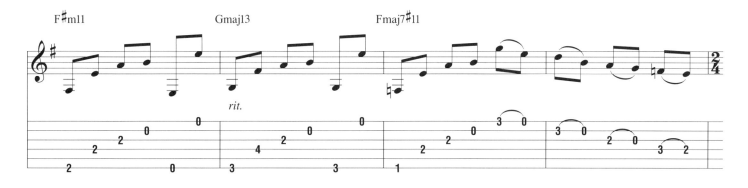

Free time

*Strum behind nut w/ R.H.

My Foolish Heart

from MY FOOLISH HEART

Words by Ned Washington
Music by Victor Young

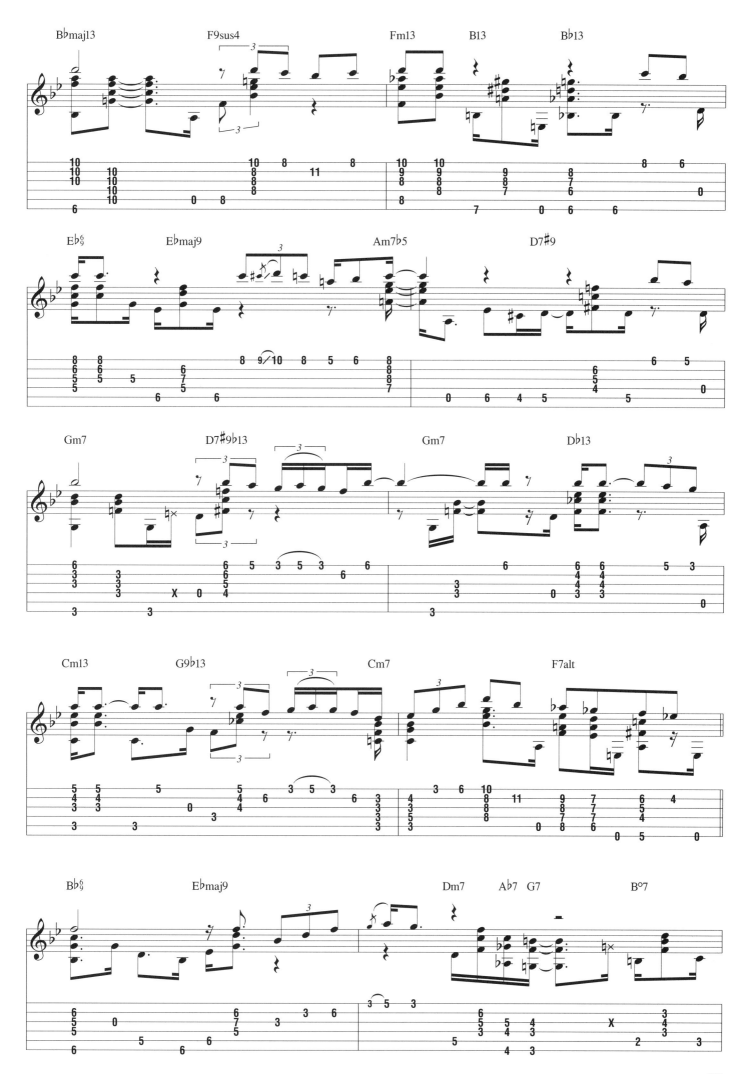

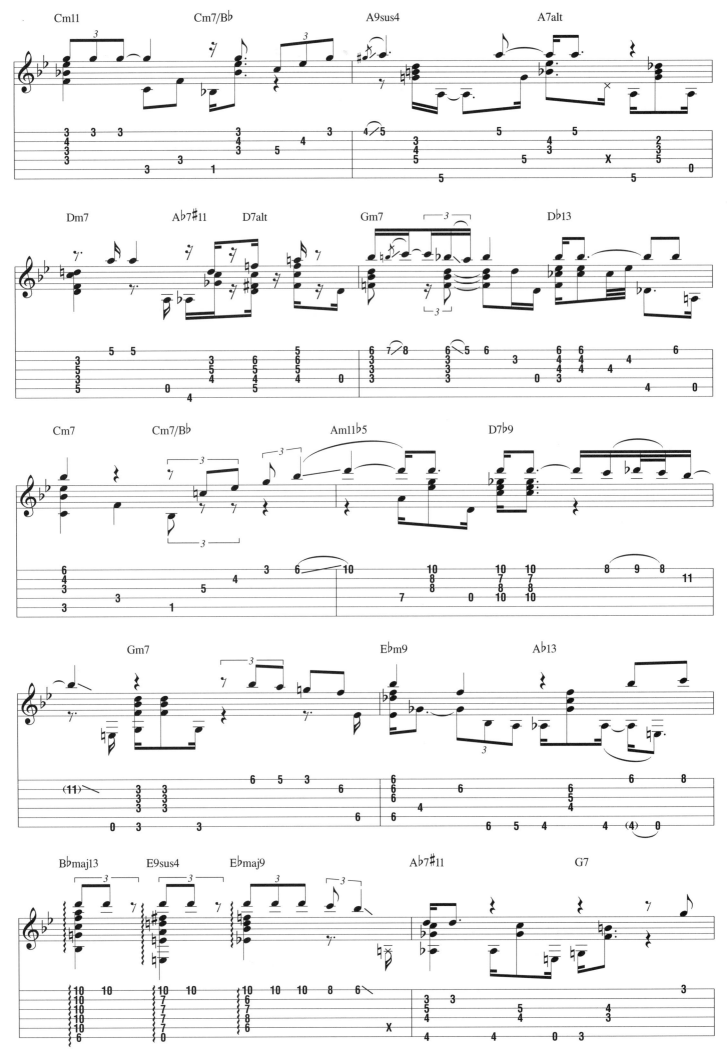

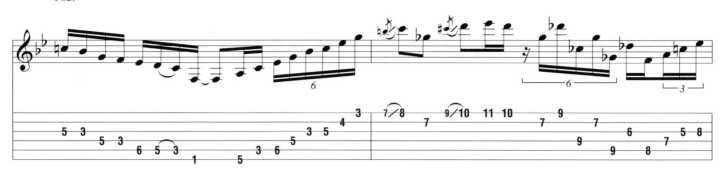

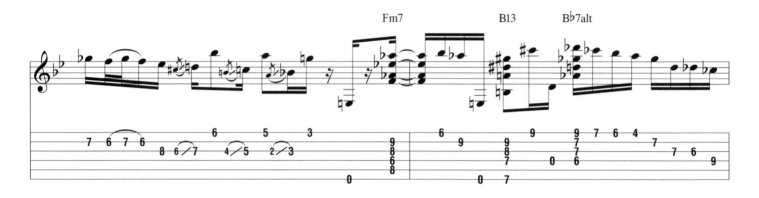

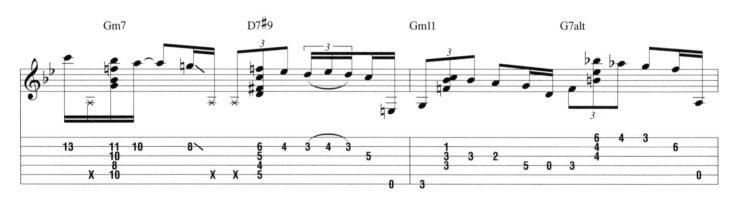

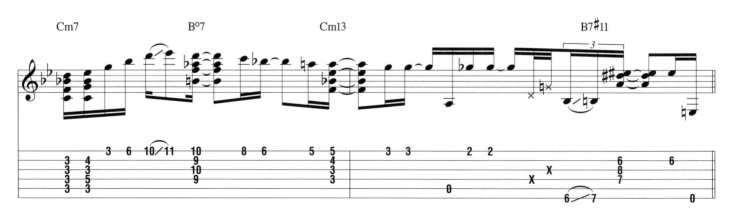

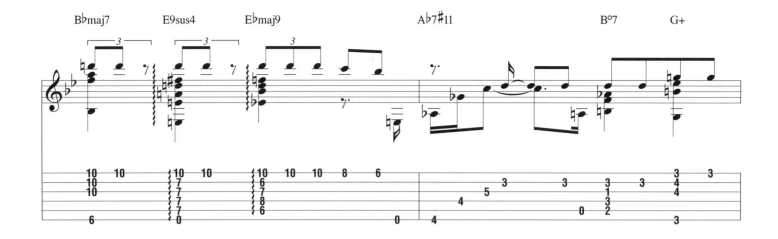

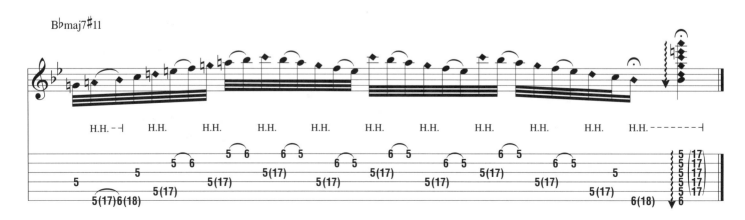

Some Enchanted Evening

from SOUTH PACIFIC
Lyrics by Oscar Hammerstein II
Music by Richard Rodgers

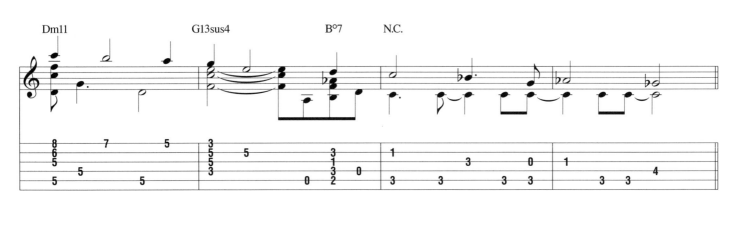

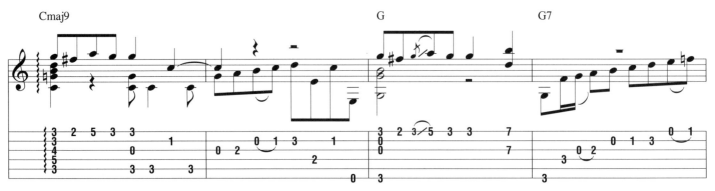

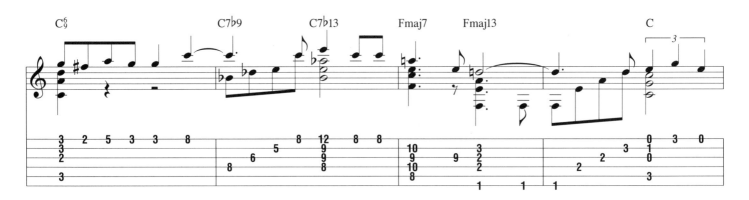

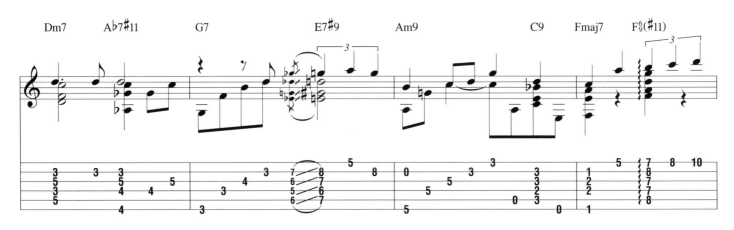

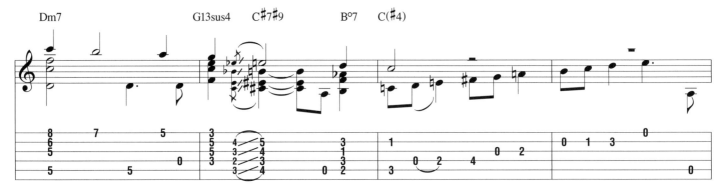

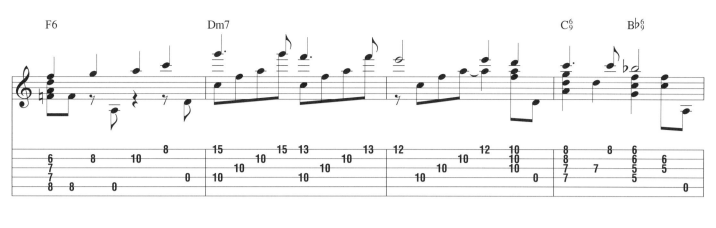

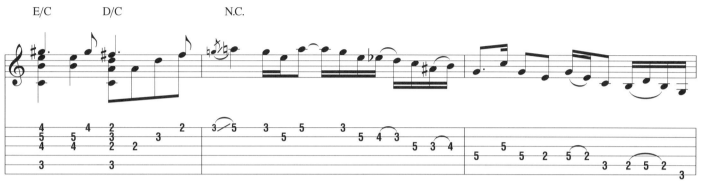

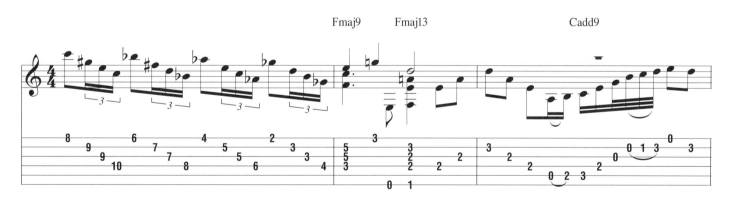

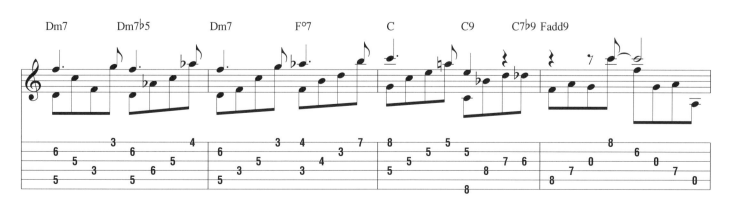

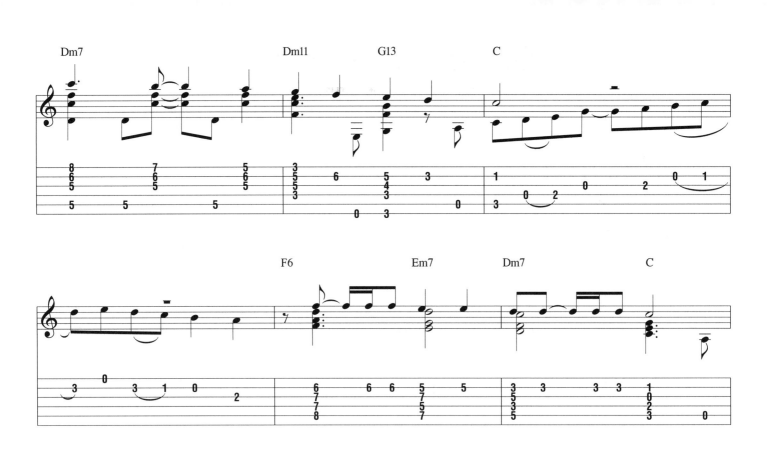

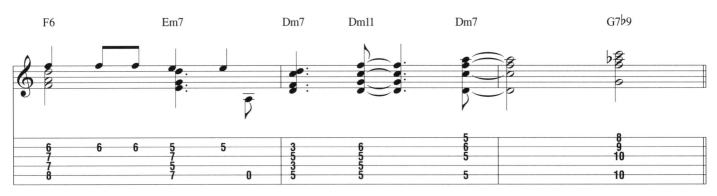

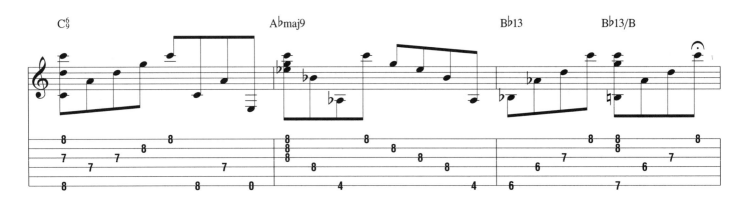

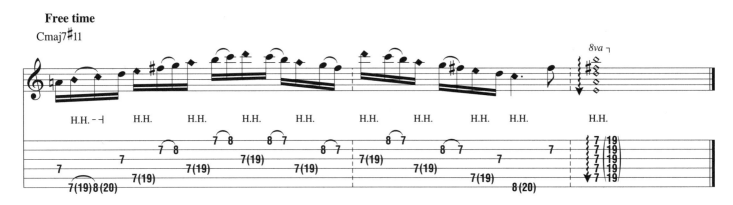

Stella by Starlight

from the Paramount Picture THE UNINVITED
Words by Ned Washington
Music by Victor Young

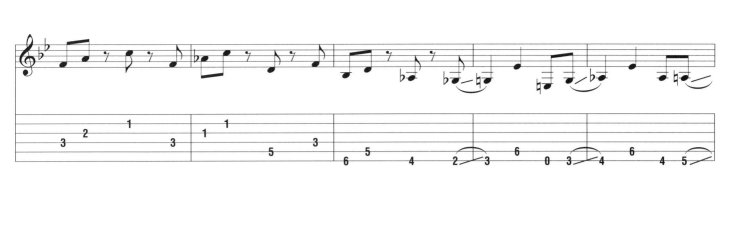

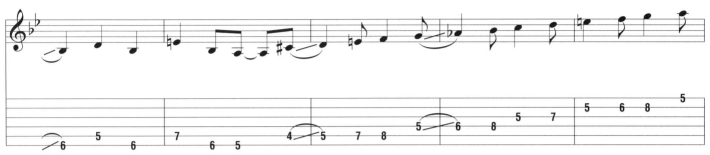

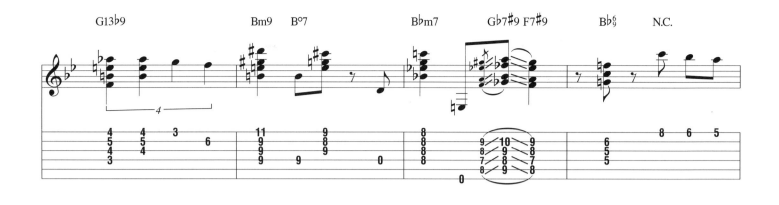

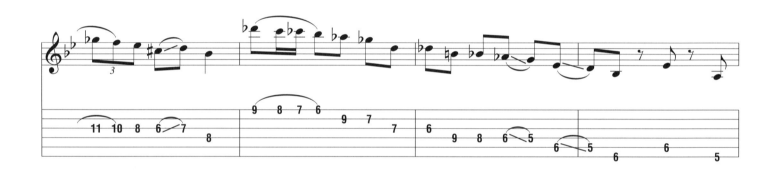

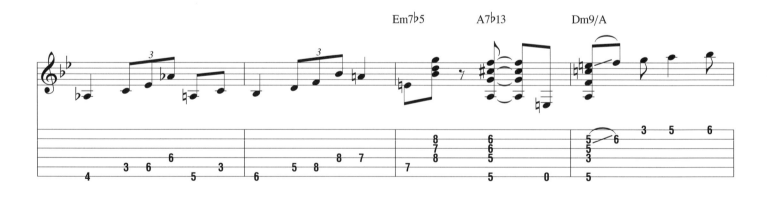

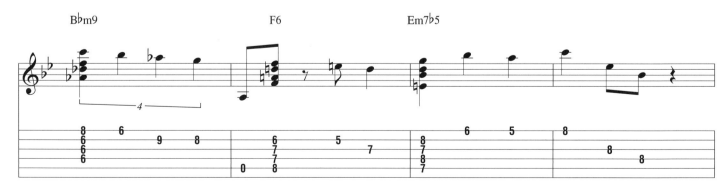

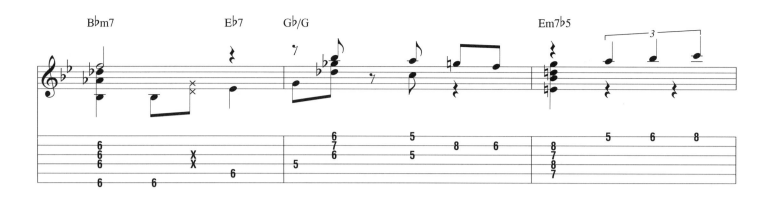

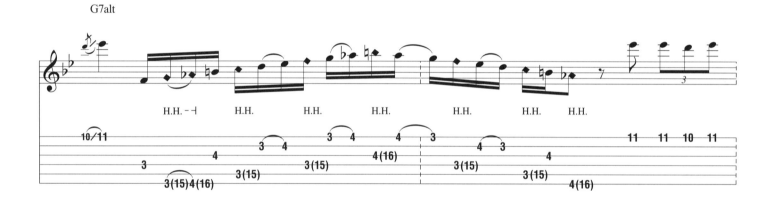

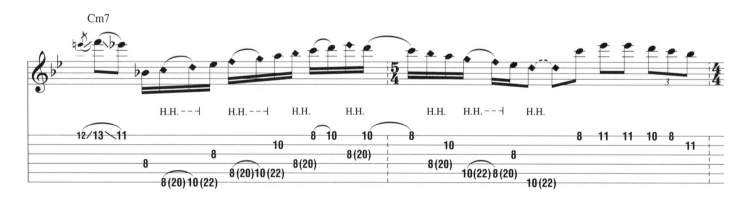

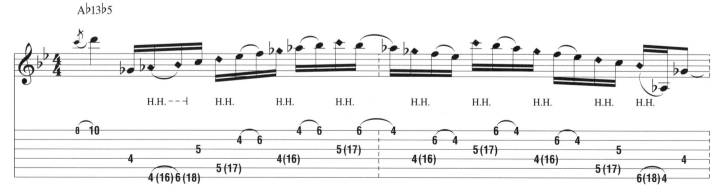

Faster

N.C.

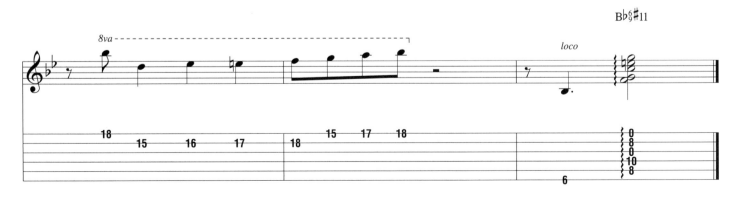

Take the "A" Train

Words and Music by Billy Strayhorn

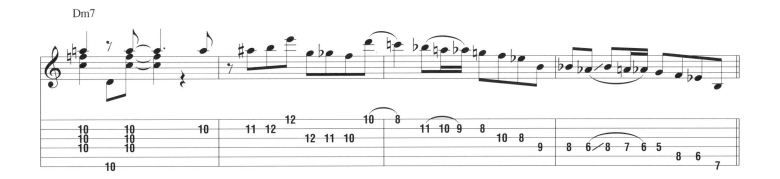

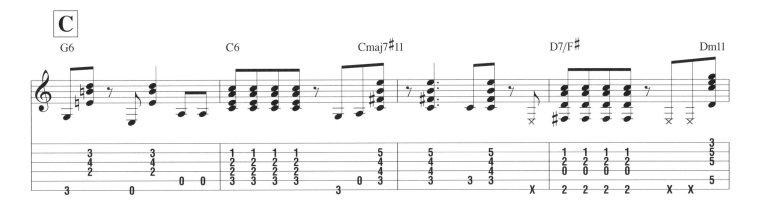

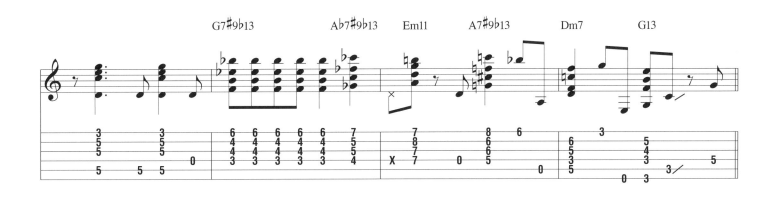

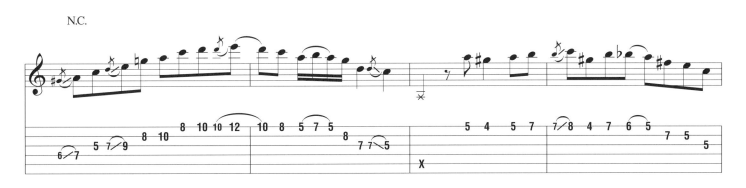

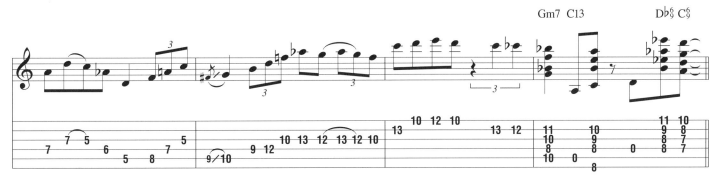

N.C.

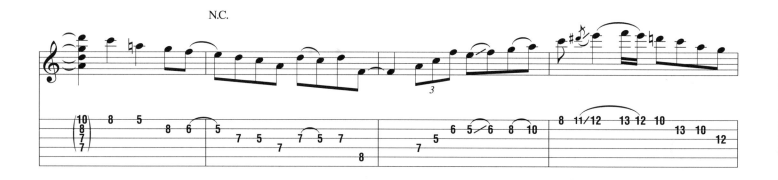

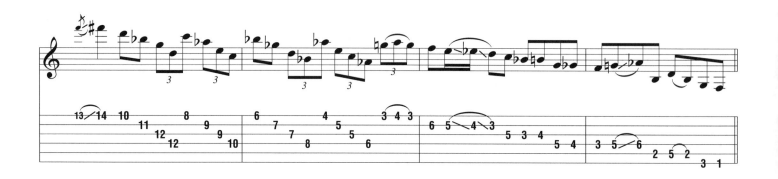

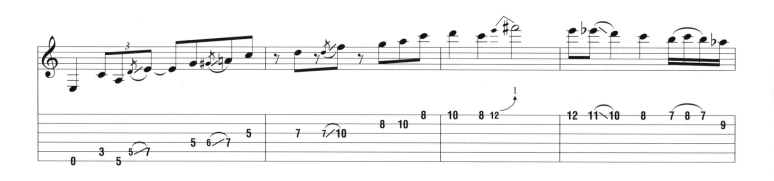

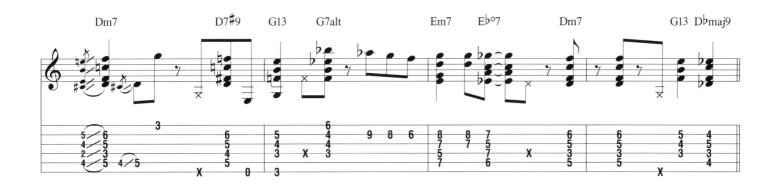

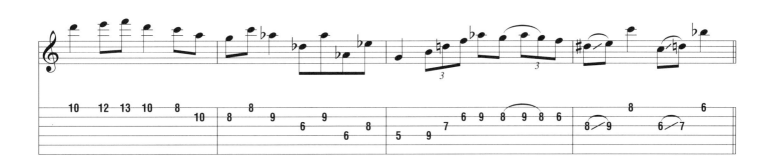

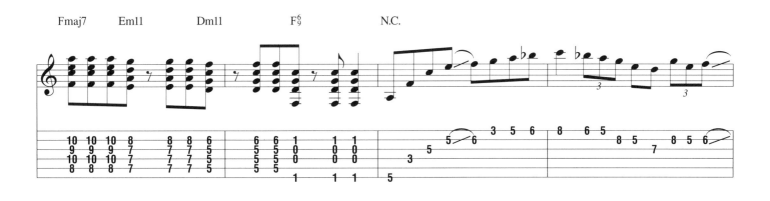

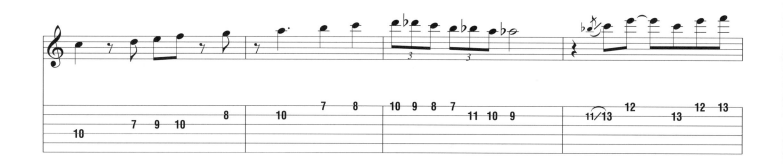

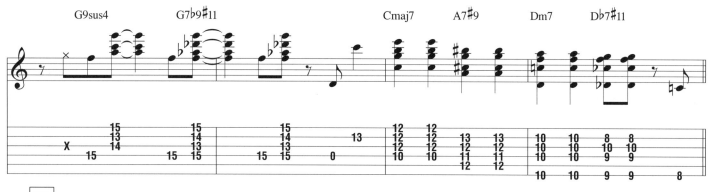

D

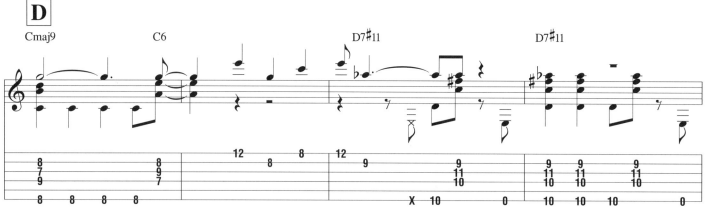

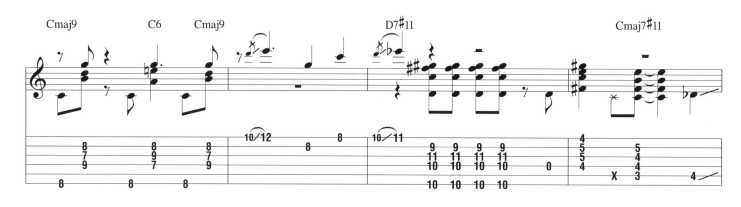

Yesterdays

from ROBERTA
from LOVELY TO LOOK AT
Words by Otto Harbach
Music by Jerome Kern

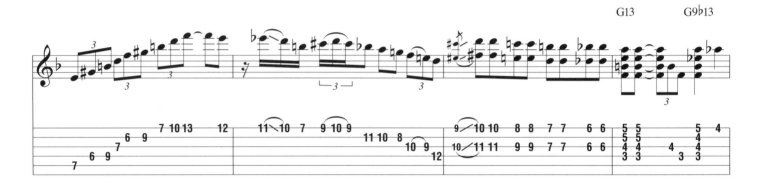

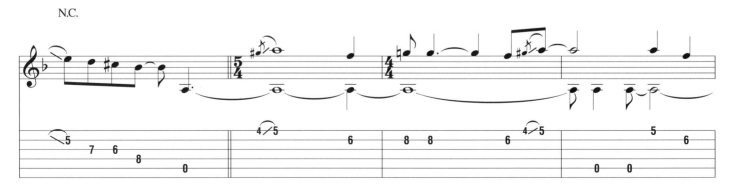

Younger Than Springtime

from SOUTH PACIFIC

Lyrics by Oscar Hammerstein II
Music by Richard Rodgers

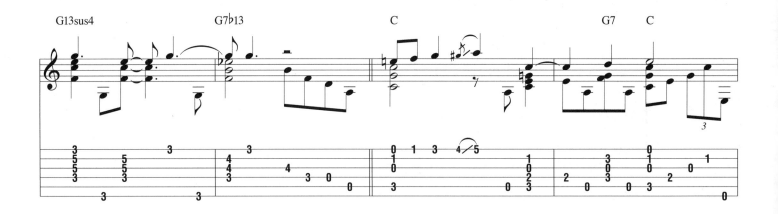

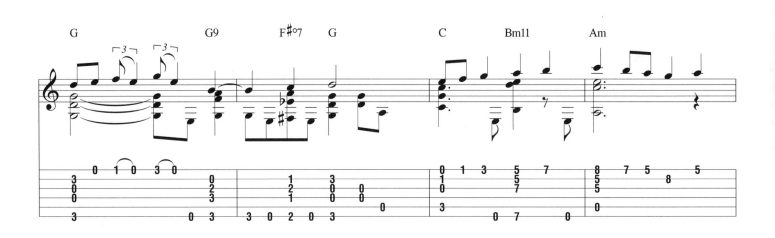

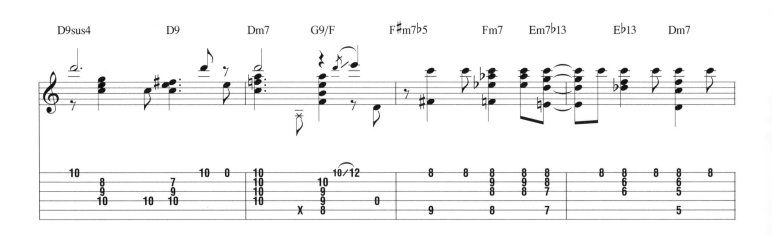

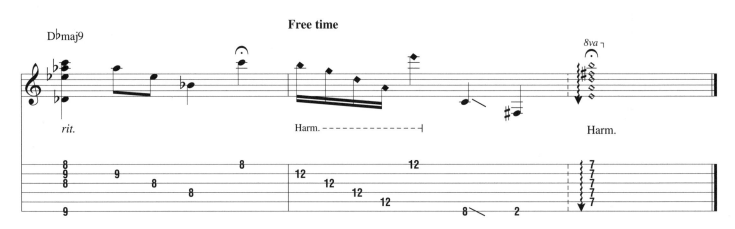